EDGE
BOOKS™

STARS OF PRO WRESTLING

CHRIS JERICHO

BY SEAN STEWART PRICE

Consultant:
Mike Johnson, Writer
PWInsider.com

Capstone
press®

Mankato, Minnesota

Edge Books are published by Capstone Press,
151 Good Counsel Drive, P.O. Box 669, Mankato, Minnesota 56002.
www.capstonepress.com
Copyright © 2010 by Capstone Press, a Capstone Publishers company.

Library of Congress Cataloging-in-Publication Data
Price, Sean.
    Chris Jericho / by Sean Stewart Price.
    p. cm. — (Edge books. Stars of pro wrestling)
    Includes bibliographical references and index.
    Summary: "Describes the life and career of pro wrestler Chris
Jericho" — Provided by publisher.
    ISBN 978-1-4296-3350-5 (library binding)
    1. Jericho, Chris — Juvenile literature. 2. Wrestlers — Canada —
Biography — Juvenile literature. I. Title.
GV1196.J47P75 2010
796.812092 — dc22
[B]   2008055906

Editorial Credits
Angie Kaelberer, editor; Ted Williams, designer; Jo Miller, media researcher

Photo Credits
Corbis Sygma/Geiger Kraig, 29
Getty Images Inc., 19; Frank Micelotta, cover, 15; Time Life Pictures/Steve
    Liss, 12; WireImage/George Pimentel, 17
Globe Photos/John Barrett, 16, 20, 23
Newscom, 5, 25; Oliver Andrivon, 6, 9; Splash News/Ronald Asadorian, 11;
    WENN/Carrie Devorah, 24; WENN/Nikki Nelson, 27
U.S. Air Force photo by Senior Airman Nicholas Pilch, 28

Design Elements
Shutterstock/amlet; Henning Janos; J. Danny; kzww

062011
006228WZVMI

TABLE OF CONTENTS

Chapter 1

RETURN OF A CHAMPION

A mysterious video greeted World Wrestling Entertainment (WWE) fans at the Bradley Center in Milwaukee, Wisconsin, on September 24, 2007. The video showed a jumble of numbers and letters. They flashed up on the screen very quickly. People could barely make out a message that read "Save_US.222."

Right away, the fans thought of Chris Jericho. The video looked like one that he had used in the past. Chris was a famous wrestler. But he had stopped competing two years before.

The guessing game ended on November 19 in Fort Lauderdale, Florida. Chris interrupted wrestler Randy Orton's speech. Fans cheered as Chris stepped back into the ring. It was like he had never been away.

Chris returned to WWE
after a two-year absence.

SAVE_US

The "Save_US" message in the video had a point. Chris said he wanted to save fans from uninteresting wrestlers like Randy Orton and Jeff Hardy. In March 2008, Chris defeated Hardy for the Intercontinental Championship. But bigger things were to come.

Shawn Michaels (center) wrestled Chris at No Mercy.

On September 7, 2008, Chris won the World Heavyweight Championship by defeating four other wrestlers in a scramble match. Shawn Michaels then challenged Chris to a ladder match at WWE's No Mercy event in October. Chris' Heavyweight title would be on the line.

NO MERCY

The Heavyweight title belt hung high above the ring. The first wrestler to climb a ladder and grab the belt would win. Michaels opened the match by slamming Chris to the mat. Chris responded by *clotheslining* Michaels to the **apron**. Chris then pulled a ladder into the ring. Michaels climbed up the ladder, and Chris knocked him down.

apron — the material covering the outer sides of a wrestling ring

WRESTLING MOVE

clothesline — a wrestler runs toward the opponent with his arm outstretched and smashes his arm into the opponent's neck

Chris and Michaels took turns dragging ladders into the ring and using them as weapons against each other. At one point, both wrestlers were on the ropes with a ladder between them. Michaels pushed the ladder on Chris, knocking him down. Michaels got ready to kick Chris in the chin. But Chris used a ladder to block Michaels' move.

Then Chris unleashed one of his **signature moves**, the *Lionsault*. Chris then pinned Michaels to the mat with a ladder. As Michaels lay there in pain, Chris climbed to the top of the ladder. Michaels then pushed the ladder off his body, sending Chris to the mat. Both wrestlers climbed to the top of the ladder. Who would reach the belt first?

signature move — the move for which a wrestler is best known

WRESTLING FACT

Chris' fans call themselves Jericholics.

Chris leaped on Michaels with a Lionsault.

WRESTLING MOVE

Lionsault — a springboard backflip off the middle rope

Chapter 2

GETTING STARTED

Chris Irvine was born November 9, 1970, to Ted and Loretta Irvine. Chris was born on Long Island, New York. But he grew up in Winnipeg, Manitoba, Canada. Chris' father was a professional hockey player. Ted played for the New York Rangers, the St. Louis Blues, and the Los Angeles Kings.

Chris played hockey himself. He also enjoyed playing baseball, football, and water polo. But Chris loved wrestling most of all. Chris started watching pro wrestling with his grandmother. He was a big fan of the American Wrestling Association (AWA).

In 2002, Chris played in a charity hockey tournament with his dad (left) and Mark Messier (center).

Wrestler Jesse Ventura gave Chris advice about the wrestling business.

CHOOSING A CAREER

In high school, Chris thought about many careers. He played bass guitar in several bands with high school friends. But Chris didn't think he was good enough to be a professional musician.

After high school, Chris attended Red River Community College in Winnipeg. He earned a two-year degree in **journalism**. He worked as a sportswriter for the *Winnipeg Free Press*. But he quickly realized that writing was not for him.

journalism — gathering and reporting news

LEARNING TO WRESTLE

As a teenager, Chris sought out pro wrestlers at wrestling events. He asked them about what wrestling was like. He also asked for advice about how to become a wrestler. One day, he talked with Jesse Ventura. Ventura told Chris that he had to learn to live every day in pain.

In June 1990, Chris enrolled in the Hart Brothers Pro Wrestling Camp in Calgary, Alberta, Canada. This school was known as one of the toughest in the wrestling business. Every day, Chris did brutal stretching and weightlifting exercises. The tough training paid off. By the time Chris graduated in September, he had gained both the moves and the endurance he would need to wrestle.

WRESTLING FACT

Chris' newspaper job taught him that he wanted a career in the spotlight. "I wanted to be the guy who was being written about," he said.

HARD TIMES

Chris had to prove he was good enough to make it in wrestling. He got jobs with small wrestling companies. But they didn't pay well. Chris had to take non-wrestling jobs to make ends meet.

During this time, Chris came up with his wrestling name. He took it from a heavy-metal song called "The Walls of Jericho" by Helloween.

On January 29, 1993, Chris won his first title. He defeated Biff Wellington to win the Canadian Heavyweight Championship. But he held the title for only two weeks.

OFF TO MEXICO

Chris soon got another job. He went to Mexico to wrestle for a company called Empressa Mejicana de Lucha Libre. In Spanish, *lucha libre* means "free fight."

In Mexico, Chris came up with his first signature move, the Lionsault. Chris used the Lionsault to win his second championship. On December 4, 1993, he defeated Mano Negra to win the National Wrestling Alliance Middleweight title in Mexico.

Chris has known Rey Mysterio Jr. (top) since his days wrestling in Mexico.

By this time, Chris was famous in Mexico. He appeared on TV wrestling shows. Fans snapped up T-shirts and trading cards with his image. Chris said he learned how to wrestle in Canada, but he learned how to be a star in Mexico.

WRESTLING FACT

Early in his career, Chris wrestled at a child's birthday party. He expected to get paid, but all he received was a hot dog and a glass of orange juice!

MOVING TO THE BIG TIME

Chris worked for the next three years in Mexico, Germany, Canada, Japan, and the United States. His fame gradually grew. So did his reputation as a good, hardworking wrestler. But Chris' goal was to work for one of the two big U.S. wrestling companies, World Championship Wrestling (WCW) or the World Wrestling Federation (WWF). Today the WWF is called World Wrestling Entertainment (WWE). In 1996, he got that chance when WCW offered him a job. Chris was about to become a big-time wrestler.

Chris worked hard to reach the top of the wrestling world.

Heel wrestlers are often on the losing end of a match.

BABYFACES AND HEELS

Wrestlers play roles in the ring. Good guys are called babyfaces, or faces. Bad guys are called heels. A heel's job is to act as nasty as possible. That makes the crowd like the babyface more. It also fires up the crowd. Like most wrestlers, Chris has been both a babyface and a heel at different times in his career.

Chapter 3

HITTING THE BIG TIME

On August 20, 1996, Chris wrestled his first WCW match. He defeated Mr. JL. His early matches went so well that within a year, Chris was wrestling in championship matches. On June 28, 1997, Chris defeated Syxx for the WCW Cruiserweight title.

For the first time, Chris earned a lot of money. Before 1996, he had never made more than $50,000 during his best year. Now he was earning $165,000 per year. He was also appearing on national TV. Some of the biggest names in wrestling worked for WCW. They included Chris' hero, Hulk Hogan.

Despite his success, Chris was restless. He was seen as a minor wrestler at WCW. Bigger stars like Hogan got most of the TV airtime. Also, the WWF was putting on the biggest, most popular wrestling shows. Chris wanted to join the WWF.

By the late 1990s, Chris wanted to leave WCW for the WWF.

Chris got the nickname "Y2J" when he joined the WWF.

FROM STAR TO SUPERSTAR

In June 1999, Chris' wish came true. WWF owner Vince McMahon signed Chris to a contract. Soon afterward, Chris was standing in the post office. He saw a clock. It was counting down to the year 2000, or "Y2K." The clock gave Chris an idea for his entrance into the WWF.

During July and early August 1999, all WWF TV shows displayed a large clock. The clock counted down the seconds until August 9, 1999. On *Raw is War* that night, wrestler The Rock was speaking in the ring. During The Rock's speech, the clock ran down to zero. Many fans didn't know what was going on. But others knew that Chris was joining the WWF. They guessed that the clock had something to do with him.

The Rock stopped his speech in mid-sentence. Fireworks exploded as Chris appeared at the entrance. Music thundered as he approached the ring. "Welcome to *Raw* is Jericho!" Chris yelled to the crowd. He told the wild crowd that he was Chris Jericho, known now as "Y2J." He was there to save the fans from boring wrestlers like The Rock.

Chris' first match was against Road Dogg Jesse James on August 26. Chris lost that match. But soon, he was winning. Chris quickly became one of the WWF's top wrestlers. Part of his appeal was his ability to outtalk his opponents. Wrestling fans love verbal feuds between wrestlers. And Chris' wrestling was as good as his speaking skills. He came up with new wrestling moves like the *Walls of Jericho*. By the end of 1999, he had won his first Intercontinental Championship by defeating Chyna.

UNDISPUTED CHAMPION

In 2001, the WWF bought WCW and combined the two companies. WWF wrestlers now had the chance to win both WWF and WCW championships. On December 9, 2001, Chris beat The Rock for the WCW Championship. He also beat Steve Austin for the WWF Championship. These victories made him the first Undisputed World Champion.

WRESTLING MOVE

Walls of Jericho — to turn the opponent facedown and grab both of his legs, bending the back and legs back toward the opponent's face

Chris kept on winning championships. He won the World Tag Team Championship twice in 2001, once with Chris Benoit and once with The Rock. In 2002, he won the title a third time with Christian. In September 2004, Chris won his seventh Intercontinental Championship.

Chris used the Walls of Jericho to defeat opponents such as The Rock.

A Break from Wrestling

In August 2005, Chris lost a match to WWE champion John Cena. Chris then disappeared from WWE's TV shows. Fans wondered if he'd ever wrestle again. But Chris was just taking a break. Chris still loved writing and performing music. During the time off, he played concerts and recorded CDs with his band, Fozzy. He also appeared on several TV shows. When Chris returned to the ring in November 2007, he was ready to wrestle.

Chris lost a match to John Cena before taking a break from WWE.

Chris worked on his music career during his time away from wrestling.

At No Mercy in 2008, Chris was determined to keep his World Heavyweight Championship. He wrestled Shawn Michaels in a ladder match. Late in the match, both Michaels and Chris were at the top of the ladder. They struggled for the belt. Chris gave Michaels a final shove as he grabbed the belt and fell to the mat. Chris remained the World Heavyweight Champion. This victory capped his comeback to the ring.

Chapter 4

THE REAL CHRIS

When he wrestles, Chris is a tough-talking, bodyslamming guy. Outside the ring, he is a soft-spoken man who likes to read books to classes of schoolchildren. Chris is also proud of his strong Christian faith.

Chris' wife is named Jessica. They have three children. Their son, Ash, was born in 2003. Their twin daughters, Cheyenne and Sierra, were born in 2006. Chris and his family live in Tampa, Florida.

Chris still has interests outside of wrestling. He has recorded CDs and played concerts with his band. Chris is also involved in movies and TV. In 2008, he hosted a musical reality show called *Redemption Song*. In 2007, he became a best-selling author with his **autobiography**, *A Lion's Tale: Around the World in Spandex*.

autobiography — a book in which the author tells about his or her life

In 2006, Chris appeared on the Video Game Awards show.

In December 2007, Chris was one of several WWE superstars who visited U.S. troops in Iraq. Chris called his trip to Iraq one of the best things he's ever done as a wrestler.

Chris is a talented man who has earned respect outside the ring. He is also a generous person who uses his time and fame to help others. No matter what happens with his wrestling career, fans are sure to hear more about him in the years ahead.

In 2007, Chris traveled to Iraq with other WWE wrestlers.

Rivals in the Ring

Wrestlers often carry on feuds with their rivals. These feuds help keep fans interested in watching the next match. Chris' first WWF feud was with Chyna. Chyna and Chris wrestled three separate times for the Intercontinental Championship. Each won a match. The third match was a tie, and they shared the title.

Chris also feuded with The Rock. Like Chris, The Rock was known for his speaking ability in the ring. Chris defeated The Rock for the WCW Championship in 2001. After he returned to WWE in 2007, Chris feuded with Shawn Michaels. Michaels interfered in a match between Chris and Kofi Kingston, causing Chris to lose. In September 2008, Chris lost a match to Michaels, but he defeated Michaels in a ladder match one month later.

The Rock (left) and Chyna (right) were two of Chris' biggest rivals.

GLOSSARY ★ ★ ★ ★ ★ ★

apron (AY-pruhn) — the material that covers the outer sides of a wrestling ring

autobiography (aw-tuh-by-AH-gruh-fee) — a book in which the author tells about his or her life

babyface (BAY-bee-fayss) — a wrestler who acts as a hero in the ring

feud (FYOOD) — a long-running quarrel between two people or groups of people

heel (HEEL) — a wrestler who acts as a villain in the ring

journalism (JUR-nuhl-iz-uhm) — the work of gathering and reporting news for newspapers, magazines, and TV

signature move (SIG-nuh-chur MOOV) — the move for which a wrestler is best known; this move is also called a finishing move.

READ MORE

Hunter, Matt. *Pro Wrestling's Greatest Matches.* Pro Wrestling Legends. Philadelphia: Chelsea House, 2001.

Schaefer, A. R. *Y2J: Pro Wrestler Chris Jericho.* Pro Wrestlers. Mankato, Minn.: Capstone Press, 2003.

Shields, Brian, and Kevin Sullivan. *WWE Encyclopedia.* New York: DK Publishing, 2009.

INTERNET SITES

FactHound offers a safe, fun way to find Internet sites related to this book. All of the sites on FactHound have been researched by our staff.

Here's all you do:

Visit *www.facthound.com*

FactHound will fetch the best sites for you!

INDEX ★ ★ ★ ★ ★ ★